For

WIT AND WISDOM
OF
FAMOUS
AMERICAN
WOMEN

Edited by
Evelyn L. Beilenson
and Ann Tenenbaum

Design by
Evelyn Loeb
and Arlene Greco

PETER PAUPER PRESS, INC.
WHITE PLAINS, NEW YORK

For Suzanne

Photographs reprinted with the permission of
FPG International.

Copyright © 1986, 1995
Peter Pauper Press, Inc.
202 Mamaroneck Avenue
White Plains, NY 10601
All rights reserved
ISBN 0-88088-157-7
Printed in China
13   12   11   10   9   8

Table of Contents

Introduction. 5

Artists, Entertainers, and Athletes 9

Writers 17

Political Participants 29

Social Activists. 37

Pioneer Spirits 45

Social Observers and Reporters. 53

Appendix 57

Introduction

"We, the people of the United States." Which "We, the people"? The women were not included.
LUCY STONE

The persons quoted in this book are all women and each one is American. At first glance, it seems that these are their only common denominators. But in fact there is a much more important connection to be discovered and understood. All of these women are, in a sense, pioneers, for they have all succeeded as women in a predominantly male society. And, perhaps of more significance, they all have possessed a very special kind of courage, the courage to persevere, even in the face of most unfavorable odds.

From Anne Hutchinson in the 17th century to Gloria Steinem in the present day, women's goals, visions, hopes, and dreams for equality and freedom have remained constant. While progress has been made since women got the vote, it is evident from the quotes that the pressures and conflicts of being female in America are far from being resolved.

It is not coincidental that forward progress for women has accompanied—and in the past 30 years has followed—progress for blacks and other minorities. Only when Americans have completed the task of eradicating all types of inequality in our society will women—along with men—have attained the goals that our foremothers envisioned.

The editors, while compiling the material for this book, became acutely aware that prior to 1960 the statements of men were widely printed while the voices of women, if heard at all, were rarely recorded. As literature reflects the attitudes of society, it is distinctly obvious that women were not taken seriously until just recently. Today's emergence of women as important and respected voices is an indication of the progress women have made toward becoming equal members of American society.

Nonetheless, because of limited space, the words of many important women have had to be omitted from this book. We hope, however, that the quotes we have chosen do reflect a balanced view of the seriousness, determination, and humor with which women have approached all aspects of their lives.

E. L. B.   A. T.

Katharine Hepburn

ARTISTS, ENTERTAINERS, AND ATHLETES

It takes great passion and great energy to do anything creative, especially in the theater. You have to care so much that you can't sleep, you can't eat, you can't talk to people. It's just got to be right. You can't do it without that passion.

AGNES DE MILLE

Some people are still unaware that reality contains unparalleled beauties. The fantastic and unexpected, the ever-changing and renewing is nowhere so exemplified as in real life itself.

BERENICE ABBOTT

Too much of a good thing can be wonderful.

MAE WEST

There's no deodorant like success.

ELIZABETH TAYLOR

Life is what we make it, always has been, always will be.

GRANDMA MOSES

I don't know what I am, dahling. I've tried several varieties of sex. The conventional position makes me claustrophobic. And the others either give me a stiff neck or lockjaw.

TALLULAH BANKHEAD

The only time a woman really succeeds in changing a man is when he is a baby.

NATALIE WOOD

For a long time the only time I felt beautiful— in the sense of being complete as a woman, as a human being, and even female—was when I was singing.

LEONTYNE PRICE

The acceptance of women as authority figures or as role models is an important step in female education. . . . It is this process of identification, respect, and then self-respect that promotes growth.

JUDY CHICAGO

I will always be grateful for my public-park beginning in tennis. One learned many bad habits in tennis, but one learned to play against all kinds of players and against all odds.

ALICE MARBLE

Be bold. If you're going to make an error, make a doozy, and don't be afraid to hit the ball.

BILLIE JEAN KING

Old age is no place for sissies.

BETTE DAVIS

Any intelligent woman who reads the marriage contract, and then goes into it, deserves all the consequences.

ISADORA DUNCAN

I saw that nothing was permanent. You don't want to possess anything that is dear to you because you might lose it.

YOKO ONO

It's gonna be a long hard drag, but we'll make it.

JANIS JOPLIN

For an actress to be a success she must have the face of Venus, the brains of Minerva, the grace of Terpsichore, the memory of Macaulay, the figure of Juno, and the hide of a rhinoceros.

ETHEL BARRYMORE

I have too many fantasies to be a housewife.
I guess I *am* a fantasy.

MARILYN MONROE

To be a good cook you have to have a love
of the good, a love of hand work, and a love
of creating. Some people like to paint
pictures, or do gardening, or build a boat in
the basement. Other people get a tremen-
dous pleasure out of the kitchen, because
cooking is just as creative and imaginative an
activity as drawing, or wood carving, or
music. And cooking draws upon your every
talent–science, mathematics, energy, history,
experience–and the more experience you
have the less likely are your experiments to
end in drivel and disaster. The more you
know, the more you can create. There's no
end to imagination in the kitchen.

JULIA CHILD

I wanted to get a quality, something like
ethereal, and I did to a point. Now I want to
carry it to a whisper. Because I think a
whisper can be stronger, an atom can be
stronger than a whole mountain.

LOUISE NEVELSON

Nobody sees a flower–really–it is so small–
we haven't time–and to see takes time like to
have a friend takes time.

GEORGIA O'KEEFFE

You grow up the day you have your first real
laugh–at yourself.

ETHEL BARRYMORE

I have everything I had twenty years ago,
only it's all a little bit lower.

GYPSY ROSE LEE

Success is important only to the extent that
it puts one in a position to do more things
one likes to do.

SARAH CALDWELL

Audiences have kept me alive.

JUDY GARLAND

For me it's the challenge–the challenge to try to beat myself or do better than I did in the past. I try to keep in mind not what I have accomplished but what I have to try to accomplish in the future.

JACKIE JOYNER-KERSEE

When I want to really blast one, I just loosen my girdle and let 'er fly.

BABE DIDRIKSON ZAHARIAS

I still want to do my work, I still want to do my livingness. And I have lived. I have been fulfilled. I recognized what I had, and I never sold it short. And I ain't through yet!

LOUISE NEVELSON

I am independent! I can live alone and I love to work.

MARY CASSATT

Willa Cather

WRITERS

Art, it seems to me, should simplify.
WILLA CATHER

Only in growth, reform and change, paradoxically enough, is true security to be found.
ANNE MORROW LINDBERGH

What a commentary on civilization, when being alone is considered suspect; when one has to apologize for it, make excuses, hide the fact that one practices it–like a secret vice.
ANNE MORROW LINDBERGH

Being an old maid is like death by drowning–a really delightful sensation after you have ceased struggling.
EDNA FERBER

I know what I wish Ralph Nader would investigate next. Marriage. It's not safe—it's not safe at all.

JEAN KERR

To reproach artists for having an insufficiently radical relation to the world has to be a complaint about art as such. And to reproach art is, in more than one way, like reproaching consciousness itself for being a burden.

SUSAN SONTAG

Quite often you want to tell somebody your dream, your nightmare. Well, nobody wants to hear about someone else's dream, good or bad; nobody wants to walk around with it. The writer is always tricking the reader into listening to the dream.

JOAN DIDION

I cannot and will not cut my conscience to fit this year's fashions.

LILLIAN HELLMAN

Money is the root of all good.

AYN RAND

Hemingway, remarks are not literature.

GERTRUDE STEIN

We are traditionally rather proud of ourselves
for having slipped creative work in there
between the domestic chores and obligations.
I'm not sure we deserve such big A-pluses for
all that.

TONI MORRISON

Give me your tired, your poor,
   Your huddled masses yearning to breathe
   free,
The wretched refuse of your teeming shore,
Send these, the homeless, tempest-tossed
   to me,
I lift my lamp beside the golden door!

EMMA LAZARUS

I like people who refuse to speak until they are ready to speak.

LILLIAN HELLMAN

If I can stop one heart from breaking,
I shall not live in vain:
If I can ease one life the aching,
Or cool one pain,
Or help one fainting robin
Unto his nest again,
I shall not live in vain.

EMILY DICKINSON

It is essential to the sanity of mankind that each one should think the other crazy–a condition with which the cynicism of human nature so cordially complies, one could wish it were a concurrence upon a subject more noble.

EMILY DICKINSON

Don't shut yourself up in a bandbox because you are a woman, but understand what is going on, and educate yourself to take part in the world's work for it all affects you and yours.

LOUISA MAY ALCOTT,
Little Women

Each story is like a new challenge or a new adventure and I don't find help anywhere, or look for it anywhere, except inside.

EUDORA WELTY

People have been writing premature obituaries on the women's movement since its beginning.

ELLEN GOODMAN

The delights of self-discovery are always available.

GAIL SHEEHY

From birth to age eighteen, a girl needs good parents. From eighteen to thirty-five, she needs good looks. From thirty-five to fifty-five, she needs a good personality. From fifty-five on, she needs good cash.

SOPHIE TUCKER

It is not healthy when a nation lives within a nation, as colored Americans are living inside America. A nation cannot live confident of its tomorrow if its refugees are among its own citizens.

PEARL S. BUCK

Deliver me from writers who say the way they live doesn't matter. I'm not sure a bad person can write a good book. If art doesn't make us better, then what on earth is it for?

ALICE WALKER

We're going to have to debunk the myth that Africa is a heaven for black people–especially black women. We've been the mule of the world there and the mule of the world here.

ALICE WALKER

I would not attack the faith of a heathen without being sure I had a better one to put in its place.

HARRIET BEECHER STOWE

People who hate trouble generally get a good deal of it.

HARRIET BEECHER STOWE

So much has been said and sung of beautiful young girls, why don't somebody wake up to the beauty of old women?

HARRIET BEECHER STOWE

Getting along with men isn't what's truly important. The vital knowledge is how to get along with a man, one man.

PHYLLIS MCGINLEY

Changing husbands is only changing troubles.

KATHLEEN NORRIS

As long as femininity is associated with ruffles and flourishes and a lack of directness and honesty . . . (women) are never praised without being patronized. Their jacket photographs are reviewed instead of their books.

ERICA JONG

Does one's integrity ever lie in what he is not able to do? I think that usually it does, for free will does not mean one will, but many wills conflicting in one man. Freedom cannot be conceived simply. It is a mystery and one which a novel, even a comic novel, can only be asked to deepen.

FLANNERY O'CONNOR

Brevity is the soul of lingerie.

DOROTHY PARKER

While we own the appointed subordination (perhaps for the sake of order in families) let us by no means acknowledge such an inferiority as would check the ardour of our endeavors to equal in all mental accomplishments the most masculine heights that when those temporary distinctions subside, we may be equally qualified to taste the full draughts of knowledge and happiness prepared for the upright of every nation and sex.

MERCY OTIS WARREN

Misfortune, and recited misfortune in especial, may be prolonged to that point where it ceases to excite pity and arouses only irritation.

DOROTHY PARKER

In his dealings with women the American husband is, after all, only an amateur. The gigolo is a professional. Whenever an amateur and a professional compete in any line of endeavor the professional is almost without exception the victor.

HELEN LAWRENSON

I speak to the black experience because that's what I know, but I'm also talking about the human condition, and what it's like to be a human being.

MAYA ANGELOU

I have spent so long erecting partitions around the part of me that writes–learning how to close the door on it when ordinary life intervenes, how to close the door on ordinary life when it's time to start writing again–that I'm not sure I could fit the two parts of me back together now.

ANNE TYLER

When alone I am not aware of my race or my sex, both in need of social contexts for definition.

MAXINE HONG KINGSTON

And I think that's important, to know how the water's gone over the dam before you start to describe it. It helps to have been over the dam yourself.

E. ANNIE PROULX

Literature must be seen in terms of the contemporary concern for survival.

LOUISE ERDRICH

I can still see, thank God. I see the mail coming, and the laundry, and friends coming. I want to keep on writing as long as I can think.

EUDORA WELTY

Far away there in the sunshine are my highest aspirations. I may not reach them, but I can look up and see their beauty, believe in them, and try to follow where they lead.

LOUISA MAY ALCOTT

Eleanor Roosevelt

POLITICAL PARTICIPANTS

In the new code of laws which I suppose it will be necessary for you to make, I desire you would remember the ladies and be more generous and favorable to them than your ancestors. Do not put such unlimited power into the hands of husbands. Remember, all men would be tyrants if they could. If particular care and attention is not paid to the ladies, we are determined to foment a rebellion, and will not hold ourselves bound by any laws in which we have no voice or representation.

ABIGAIL ADAMS

I very sincerely wish you would exert your self so as to keep all your matters in order your self without depending upon others as that is the only way to be happy to have all your business in your one hands.

MARTHA WASHINGTON

My spirits, which I have kept up during my being drove about from place to place, much better than most people's I meet with, have been lowered by nothing but the depreciation of the money. . . . It is indeed, as you say, that money is too cheap; for there are so many people that are not used to have it, nor know the proper use of it, that get so much, that they care not whether they give one dollar or a hundred for any thing they want; but to those whose every dollar is the same as a silver one, which is our case, it is particularly hard. . . .

SARAH BACHE
Benjamin Franklin's daughter

I would rather fight with my hands than my tongue.

DOLLEY MADISON

As a woman I can't go to war, and I refuse to send anyone else.

JEANNETTE RANKIN

It's better to light a candle than to curse the darkness.

ELEANOR ROOSEVELT

I think if the people of this country can be reached with the truth, their judgment will be in favor of the many, as against the privileged few.

ELEANOR ROOSEVELT

I'm having trouble managing the mansion. What I need is a wife.

ELLA T. GRASSO

You've got to be willing to stay committed to someone over the long run, and sometimes it doesn't work out. But often if you become real honest with yourself and honest with each other, and put aside whatever personal hurt and disappointment you have to really understand yourself and your spouse, it can be the most wonderful experience you'll ever have.

HILLARY RODHAM CLINTON

Most of man's problems upon this planet, in the long history of the race, have been met and solved either partially or as a whole by experiment based on common sense and carried out with courage.

FRANCES PERKINS

Strength, the American way, is not manifested by threats of criminal prosecution or police state methods. Leadership is not manifested by coercion, even against the resented. Greatness is not manifested by unlimited pragmatism, which places such a high premium on the end justifying any means and any methods.

MARGARET CHASE SMITH

Being away from home gave me a chance to look at myself with a jaundiced eye. I learned not to be ashamed of a real hunger for knowledge, something I had always tried to hide, and I came home glad to start in here again but with a love for Europe that I am afraid will never leave me.

JACQUELINE KENNEDY ONASSIS

A politician should be born a foundling and
remain a bachelor.

LADY BIRD JOHNSON

The public servant who stands on the higher
eminences of thought does not confuse the
public interest with private interest. Her or
his motivating ideal is selflessness and an
ever-present awareness of our government's
source of authority–the people. This public
servant honors American ideals by actualizing
rather than simply mouthing them and rec-
ognizes that this country's original principles
are sound.

BARBARA JORDAN

I'll have to have a room of my own. Nobody
could sleep with Dick. He wakes up during
the night, switches on the lights, speaks into
his tape recorder.

PAT NIXON

When you're in your 90's and looking back, it's not going to be how much money you made or how many awards you've won. It's really what did you stand for. Did you make a positive difference for people?

ELIZABETH DOLE

Sometimes when I look at all my children, I say to myself, "Lillian, you should have stayed a virgin."

LILLIAN CARTER

Congress is a middle-aged, middle-class, white male power structure. . . . No wonder it's been so totally unresponsive to the needs of this country.

BELLA ABZUG

I don't have easy answers for my daughter and all the others contemplating a family. Keep control of your professional life. If you determine your own schedule, life will be much easier. Be patient with your career and know the special, devoted attention a young child demands will eventually pay off.

DIANNE FEINSTEIN

I don't believe we can have justice without caring, or caring without justice. These are inseparable aspects of life and work for children as they are for adults.

JUSTINE WISE POLIER

I empathize with those who yearn for a simpler world—for some bygone golden age of domestic and international tranquility.
Perhaps for a few people at some time in history there was such an age. But for the mass of humanity it is an age that never was.

SHIRLEY HUFSTEDLER

Censorship, like charity, should begin at home; but unlike charity, it should end there.

CLARE BOOTHE LUCE

I have a brain and a uterus and I use them both.

PATRICIA SCHROEDER

Susan B. Anthony and Elizabeth Cady Stanton

SOCIAL ACTIVISTS

The true republic—men, their rights and nothing more; women, their rights and nothing less.

SUSAN B. ANTHONY

"We, the people of the United States." Which "We, the people"? The women were not included.

LUCY STONE

It is not Christianity, but priestcraft that has subjected woman as we find her.

LUCRETIA MOTT

I said that the standards for brides are so low that a man wouldn't marry a woman he'd hire to work in his office. Because he's only been taught to look for a housekeeper and a mistress.

GLORIA STEINEM

Social science affirms that a woman's place in society marks the level of civilization.

ELIZABETH CADY STANTON

I had reasoned this out in my mind, there was two things I had a right to, liberty and death. If I could not have one, I would have the other, for no man should take me alive.

HARRIET TUBMAN

Who, I ask you, can take, dare take, on himself the rights, the duties, the responsibilities of another human soul?

ELIZABETH CADY STANTON

There is no hope even that woman, with her right to vote, will ever purify politics.

EMMA GOLDMAN

We hold these truths to be self-evident: that all men and women are created equal; that they are endowed by their Creator with certain inalienable rights; that among these are life, liberty, and the pursuit of happiness . . .
Declaration of Sentiments and Resolutions,
Seneca Falls, New York, 1848

If a woman is really injured by her marriage she should sue under the employer liability act. She should claim damages–not alimony.
CHARLOTTE PERKINS GILMAN

It is the duty of youth to bring its fresh new powers to bear on Social progress. Each generation of young people should be to the world like a vast reserve force to a tired army. They should lift the world forward. That is what they are for.
CHARLOTTE PERKINS GILMAN

If the first woman God ever made was strong enough to turn the world upside down all alone, these women together ought to be able to turn it back, and get it right side up again! And now they is asking to do it, the men better let them.

SOJOURNER TRUTH

The most far-reaching social development of modern times is the revolt of woman against sex servitude. The most important force in the remaking of the world is a free motherhood.

MARGARET SANGER

I think that implicit in the women's movement is the idea that women will share in the economic burden, and men will share more equally in the home and the family.

BETTY FRIEDAN

If our people are to fight their way up out of bondage we must arm them with the sword and the shield and the buckler of pride.

MARY MCLEOD BETHUNE

The new demand of women for political enfranchisement comes at a time when unsatisfactory and degraded social conditions are held responsible for so much wretchedness and when the fate of all the unfortunate, the suffering and the criminal is daily forced upon woman's attention in painful and intimate ways.

JANE ADDAMS

Perhaps well-to-do women and unemployed ghetto teenagers have something in common. Neither group has been allowed to develop the self-confidence that comes from knowing you can support yourself.

GLORIA STEINEM

Now, we are becoming the men we wanted to marry. Once women were trained to marry a doctor, not be one.

GLORIA STEINEM

If a law commands me to sin *I will break it;* if it calls me to suffer, I will let it take its course *unresistingly.* The doctrine of blind obedience and unqualified submission to any human power, whether civil or ecclesiastical, is the doctrine of despotism, and ought to have no place 'mong Republicans and Christians.

ANGELINA GRIMKÉ

Here then I plant myself. God created us equal;–he created us free agents;–he is our Lawgiver, our King and our Judge, and to him alone is woman bound to be in subjection, and to him alone is she accountable for the use of those talents with which her Heavenly Father has entrusted her. . . .

SARAH GRIMKÉ

The business of the husbandman is not to waste his endeavors in seeking to make his orchard attain the strength and majesty of his forest, but to rear each to the perfection of its nature.

EMMA HART WILLARD

Genuine learning has ever been said to give polish to man; why then should it not bestow added charms on women?

EMMA HART WILLARD

It is truly sorrowful to find so much suffering through neglect, ignorance, and mismanagement, but I hope for better things at no distant time. The weather has been severe and stormy, but in proportion as my own discomfort has increased, my conviction of necessity of search into the wants of the friendless and afflicted has deepened. If I am cold, they, too are cold. If I am weary, they are distressed; if I am alone, they are abandoned.

DOROTHEA DIX

There is a great stir about coloured men getting their rights but not a word about coloured women; and if coloured men get their rights and not coloured women theirs, you see, coloured men will be masters over the women. . . . I wish woman to have her voice.

SOJOURNER TRUTH

Helen Keller

PIONEER SPIRITS

Pray for the dead and fight like hell for the living.

"MOTHER" MARY JONES

I asked a man in prison once how he happened to be there and he said he had stolen a pair of shoes. I told him if he had stolen a railroad he would be a United States Senator.

"MOTHER" MARY JONES

I do not believe in sex distinction in literature, law, politics, or trade—or that modesty and virtue are more becoming to women than to men, but wish we had more of it everywhere.

BELVA LOCKWOOD

The intellect, no more than the sense of hearing is to be cultivated [not] merely that Woman may be a more valuable companion to Man but because the Power who gave a power, by its mere existence signifies that it must be brought out toward perfection. . . . Let it not be said wherever there is energy of creative genius [that] she has a masculine mind.

MARGARET FULLER

[My whole life was] devoted unreservedly to the service of my sex. The study and practice of medicine is, in my thought, but one means to a great end, for which my very soul yearns with intensest passionate emotion. . . . the true ennoblement of woman, the full harmonious development of her unknown nature, and the consequent redemption of the whole human race.

DR. ELIZABETH BLACKWELL

Adventure is worthwhile in itself.

AMELIA EARHART

I have long felt that the trouble with discrimination is not discrimination per se but rather that the people who are discriminated against think of themselves as second-class.

ROSALYN YALOW

I may be compelled to face danger, but never fear it, and while our soldiers can stand and fight, I can stand and feed and nurse them.

CLARA BARTON

Love is something like the clouds that were in the sky before the sun came out. You cannot touch the clouds, you know; but you feel the rain and know how glad the flowers and the thirsty earth are to have it after a hot day. You cannot touch love either; but you feel the sweetness that it pours into everything. Without love you would not be happy or want to play.

ANNIE SULLIVAN

Money has nothing to do with style at all, but naturally it helps every situation.

DIANA VREELAND

I say to evoke the imagination of the public is a wonderful thing if you can manage it.

DIANA VREELAND

Beauty has nothing to do with possession. If possession and beauty must go together, then we are lost souls, a beautiful flower is not there to be possessed, it's there to be beheld. You're not going to take a beautiful painting off a museum wall. It's there for your pleasure.

DIANA VREELAND

Entire species of animals have been exterminated, or reduced to so small a remnant that their survival is doubtful. Forests have been despoiled by uncontrolled and excessive cutting of lumber; grasslands have been destroyed by overgrazing. . . . We have much to accomplish before we can feel assured of passing on to future generations a land as richly endowed in natural wealth as the one we live in.

RACHEL CARSON

It was never in my heart to slight any man,
but only that man should be kept in his place
and not sit in the room of God.

ANNE HUTCHINSON

When indeed shall we learn that we are all
related one to the other, that we are all members of one body? Until the spirit of love for
our fellowmen, regardless of race, color or
creed, shall fill the world, making real in our
lives and our deeds the actuality of human
brotherhood–until the great mass of the people shall be filled with the sense of responsi-
bility for each other's welfare, social justice
can never be attained.

HELEN KELLER

Any teacher can take a child to the class-
room, but not every teacher can make him
learn. He will not work joyously unless he
feels that liberty is his, whether he is busy or
at rest; he must feel the flush of victory and
the heart-sinking of disappointment before he
takes with a will the tasks distasteful to him
and resolves to dance his way bravely
through a dull routine of textbooks.

HELEN KELLER

What if in my waking hours a sound should ring through the silent halls of hearing? What if a ray of light should flash through the darkened chambers of my soul? What would happen, I ask many and many a time. Would the bow-and-string tension of life snap? Would the heart, overweighted with sudden joy, stop beating for very excess of happiness?

HELEN KELLER

Having family responsibilities and concerns just has to make you a more understanding person.

SANDRA DAY O'CONNOR

If you ever have a new idea, and it's really new, you have to expect that it won't be widely accepted immediately. It's a long hard process.

ROSALYN YALOW

I believe one thing: that today is yesterday
and tomorrow is today and you can't stop.
The body is your instrument in dance, but
your art is outside that creature, the body. I
don't leap or jump anymore. I look at young
dancers, and I am envious, more aware of
what glories the body contains. But sensitivity
is not made dull by age.

MARTHA GRAHAM

Matter and death are mortal illusions.

MARY BAKER EDDY

Margaret Mead

SOCIAL OBSERVERS
AND REPORTERS

Great cities are not like towns, only larger.
They differ from towns and suburbs in basic
ways, and one of these is that cities are, by
definition, full of strangers.

JANE JACOBS

No matter how many communes anybody
invents, the family always creeps back.

MARGARET MEAD

To feel valued, to know, even if only once in
a while, that you can do a job well is an
absolutely marvelous feeling.

BARBARA WALTERS

Our faith in the present dies out long before
our faith in the future.

RUTH BENEDICT

It is the personality of the mistress that the home expresses. Men are forever guests in our homes, no matter how much happiness they may find there.

ELSIE DE WOLFE

The prerequisite for making love is to like someone enormously.

HELEN GURLEY BROWN

Drying a widow's tears is one of the most dangerous occupations known to man.

DOROTHY DIX

If American men are obsessed with money, American women are obsessed with weight. The men talk of gain, the women talk of loss, and I do not know which talk is the more boring.

MARYA MANNES

All judgment, I think in almost anything, even in your own personal life, grows out of being able to measure one thing against another. You measure your own judgments, you measure your own values against things that have happened to you. And you measure the value of an art against things that have happened in that art in the past. Every creative act draws on the past whether it pretends to or not. It draws on what it knows. There's no such thing, really, as a creative act in a vacuum.

ADA LOUISE HUXTABLE

You can't be too rich or too thin.

WALLIS SIMPSON, DUCHESS OF WINDSOR

Implicitly adopting the male life as the norm, they have tried to fashion women out of a masculine cloth. It all goes back, of course, to Adam and Eve–a story which shows among other things that if you make a woman out of a man, you are bound to get into trouble. In the life cycle, as in the garden of Eden, woman has been the deviant.

CAROL GILLIGAN

The sexual oppression of black women is not only an end in itself, it is also an instrument in the oppression of the entire race.

GERDA LERNER

In recent years many legal and educational barriers to female achievement have been removed; but it is clear that a psychological barrier remains. The motive to avoid success has an all-too-important influence on the intellectual and professional lives of women in our society. But perhaps there is cause for optimism.

MATINA HORNER

A job is not a career. I think I started out with a job. It turned into a career and changed my life. A career means long hours, travel, frustration and plain hard work and finally perhaps a realization that you can't have it all.

BARBARA WALTERS

APPENDIX

Abbott, Berenice (1898-1991)
    Photographer 9
Abzug, Bella (1920-)
    Former Member of Congress 34
Adams, Abigail (1744-1818)
    Author, Wife of John Adams 29
Addams, Jane (1860-1935)
    Social Reformer 41
Alcott, Louisa May (1832-1888)
    Author 21, 27
Angelou, Maya (1928-)
    Poet, Author 26
Anthony, Susan B. (1820-1906)
    Suffragette 37
Bache, Sarah (1743-1808)
    Benjamin Franklin's Daughter 30
Bankhead, Tallulah (1903-1968)
    Actress 10
Barrymore, Ethel (1879-1959)
    Actress 12, 14
Barton, Clara (1821-1912)
    Nurse 47
Benedict, Ruth (1887-1948)
    Anthropologist 53
Bethune, Mary McLeod (1875-1955)
    Educator 40
Blackwell, Dr. Elizabeth (1821-1910)
    Physician 46

Brown, Helen Gurley (1922-   )
    Editor, Author 54
Buck, Pearl S. (1892-1973)
    Author 22
Caldwell, Sarah (1924-   )
    Conductor 14
Carson, Rachel (1907-1964)
    Environmentalist 48
Carter, Lillian (1898-1983)
    Nurse, Mother of Jimmy Carter 34
Cassatt, Mary (1844-1926)
    Painter 15
Cather, Willa (1873-1947)
    Author 17
Chicago, Judy (1939-   )
    Artist 11
Child, Julia (1912-   )
    Chef, Author 13
Clinton, Hillary Rodham (1947-   )
    Wife of Bill Clinton 31
Davis, Bette (1908-1989)
    Actress 11
De Mille, Agnes (1908-1993)
    Choreographer 9
De Wolfe, Elsie (1865-1950)
    Interior Decorator 54
Dickinson, Emily (1830-1886)
    Poet 20
Didion, Joan (1925-   )
    Author, Journalist 18
Dix, Dorothea (1802-1887)
    Social Reformer 43

Dix, Dorothy (1861-1951)
Journalist 54
Dole, Elizabeth (1936-)
Former Cabinet Officer 34
Duncan, Isadora (1878-1927)
Dancer 12
Earhart, Amelia (1898-1937)
Aviatrix 46
Eddy, Mary Baker (1821-1910)
Theologian 51
Erdrich, Louise (1954-)
Author 27
Feinstein, Dianne (1933-)
U. S. Senator 34
Ferber, Edna (1887-1968)
Author 17
Friedan, Betty (1921-)
Feminist Author 40
Fuller, Margaret (1810-1850)
Feminist 46
Garland, Judy (1922-1969)
Singer, Actress 15
Gilligan, Carol (1936-)
Feminist Author 55
Gilman, Charlotte Perkins (1860-1935)
Social Critic 39
Goldman, Emma (1869-1940)
Anarchist 38
Goodman, Ellen (1941-)
Columnist 21
Graham, Martha (1894-1991)
Dancer, Choreographer 51

Grandma Moses (1860-1961)
Painter 10
Grasso, Ella T. (1919-1961)
Governor of Connecticut 31
Grimké, Angelina (1805-1879)
Abolitionist, Suffragette 42
Grimké, Sarah (1792-1873)
Abolitionist, Suffragette 42
Hellman, Lillian (1906-1984)
Dramatist, Author 18, 20
Horner, Matina (1929-   )
Psychologist 56
Hufstedler, Shirley (1925-   )
Former Secretary of Education 35
Hutchinson, Anne (1591-1642)
Social Critic 49
Huxtable, Ada Louise (1921-   )
Architectural Critic 55
Jacobs, Jane (1916-   )
Social Critic 53
Johnson, Lady Bird (1912-   )
Wife of Lyndon B. Johnson 33
Jones, "Mother" Mary (1830-1930)
Labor Leader 45
Jong, Erica (1943-   )
Poet, Author 24
Joplin, Janis (1943-1970)
Singer 12
Jordan, Barbara (1936-   )
Former Congresswoman 33
Joyner-Kersee, Jackie (1962-   )
Athlete 15

Keller, Helen (1880-1968)
Teacher, Author 49, 50
Kerr, Jean (1923-   )
Dramatist, Author 18
King, Billie Jean (1943-   )
Tennis Player 11
Kingston, Maxine Hong (1940-   )
Author 26
Lawrenson, Helen (1907-1982)
Author 25
Lazarus, Emma (1849-1887)
Poet 19
Lee, Gypsy Rose (1914-1970)
Strip Tease Artist, Author 14
Lerner, Gerda (1920-   )
Historian, Author 56
Lindbergh, Anne Morrow (1906-   )
Author 17
Lockwood, Belva (1830-1917)
Lawyer 45
Luce, Clare Boothe (1903-1987)
Diplomat, Politician 35
Madison, Dolley (1768-1849)
Wife of James Madison 30
Mannes, Marya (1904-1990)
Journalist, Critic 54
Marble, Alice (1913-   )
Tennis Player 11
McGinley, Phyllis (1905-1978)
Poet, Author 23
Mead, Margaret (1901-1978)
Anthropologist 53

Monroe, Marilyn (1926-1962)
  Actress 13
Morrison, Toni (1931-)
  Author 19
Mott, Lucretia (1793-1880)
  Suffragette 37
Nevelson, Louise (1900-1988)
  Artist 13, 15
Nixon, Pat (1912-1993)
  Wife of Richard M. Nixon 33
Norris, Kathleen (1890-1966)
  Author 24
O'Connor, Flannery (1925-1964)
  Author 24
O'Connor, Sandra Day (1930-)
  Supreme Court Justice 50
O'Keeffe, Georgia (1887-1986)
  Artist 14
Onassis, Jacqueline Kennedy (1929-1994)
  Wife of John F. Kennedy 32
Ono, Yoko (1933-)
  Musician, Wife of John Lennon 12
Parker, Dorothy (1893-1967)
  Author, Humorist 24, 25
Perkins, Frances (1882-1965)
  Secretary of Labor 32
Polier, Justine Wise (1903-1987)
  Judge 35
Price, Leontyne (1927-)
  Opera Singer 10
Proulx, E. Annie (1935-)
  Author 26

Rand, Ayn (1905-1982)
    Author 19
Rankin, Jeannette (1880-1973)
    First Woman Elected to Congress 30
Roosevelt, Eleanor (1884-1962)
    Humanitarian, UN Delegate 31
Sanger, Margaret (1883-1966)
    Social Reformer 40
Schroeder, Patricia (1940-)
    Congresswoman 35
Sheehy, Gail (1937-)
    Journalist 21
Simpson, Wallis (1896-1986)
    Duchess of Windsor 55
Smith, Margaret Chase (1897-)
    Congresswoman, Senator 32
Sontag, Susan (1933-)
    Author, Critic 18
Stanton, Elizabeth Cady (1815-1902)
    Suffragette 38
Stein, Gertrude (1874-1946)
    Author 19
Steinem, Gloria (1934-)
    Feminist, Author 37, 41
Stone, Lucy (1818-1893)
    Suffragette 37
Stowe, Harriet Beecher (1811-1896)
    Author 23
Sullivan, Annie (1866-1936)
    Teacher 47
Taylor, Elizabeth (1932-)
    Actress 10

Truth, Sojourner (1797-1883)
    Suffragette, Abolitionist 40, 43
Tubman, Harriet (1820-1913)
    Abolitionist, Liberator 38
Tucker, Sophie (1884-1966)
    Entertainer 22
Tyler, Anne (1941-   )
    Author 26
Vreeland, Diana (1903?-1989)
    Fashion Editor 47, 48
Walker, Alice (1933-   )
    Author 22
Walters, Barbara (1931-   )
    Broadcast Journalist 53, 56
Warren, Mercy Otis (1728-1814)
    Dramatist, Poet 25
Washington, Martha (1732-1802)
    Wife of George Washington 29
Welty, Eudora (1909-   )
    Author 21, 27
West, Mae (1892-1980)
    Actress 9
Willard, Emma Hart (1787-1870)
    Educator 42, 43
Wood, Natalie (1938-1981)
    Actress 10
Yalow, Rosalyn (1921-   )
    Physicist 47, 50
Zaharias, Babe Didrikson (1914-1956)
    Athlete 15